The Audacious Dreamer

A story of faith, hope and love

PERIS MBUTHIA

To my family:
My rock and best friend hubby Martin Mbuthia,
and beautiful daughters Sandra and Maxine.
You are the greatest gift God gave me. I love you.

Acknowledgments

IT HAS TAKEN A LOT of love, kindness and patience for this book to come to life. First and foremost I would like to thank God for giving me the power to believe in my passion and pursue my dreams. I could never have done this without the faith I have in you God. I thank my mum and dad without whom there would be no me and consequently this book wouldn't have come to fruition. My siblings; I could not have chosen a better family, maybe I would have tried when we were younger but I would have failed miserably!

To my friends; especially Anthony Gitonga, who played a key role in urging me and guiding me towards my journey to writing this book, may God bless you.

To my spiritual father, Pastor Lennox John, thank you for all your prayers. To my Amway mentors; Sid & Rup, Vishal & Zeenia and Alvind & poonum; thank you for inspiring and showing me how to balance work-life.

To Kenya my birth home, I love you and to Canada my adoptive country, you're the best; there is no clash when it comes to you two.

And lastly to my editor Esther Kiragu who assisted me to bring this book to realization; thank you, we did great!

Table of Contents

To accomplish great things, we must not only dream, but also act; not only plan, but also have two choices: to continue to sleep with dreams or to wake up and chase them.

Introduction

You can dream again.

The minute you settle for less than you deserve,
you get less than you settled for.
– Maureen Dowd

NEVER BEFORE DID I ENVISAGE myself writing a book. Writing always felt like a distant dream for some other time and people. But in the course of my life I have interacted and counseled with many and part of my life story has always come in handy to inspire and instruct those who seek my opinion.

This especially became evident when I set up my business; Timeless Medical Spa in Nairobi. In my interaction with clients, many of them continue to mention how inspiring I am to them and that they always leave my office not just with a relaxing spa treatment but also with uplifted hearts.

I especially recall a conversation I had in June 2017 with a client and a friend over a cup of coffee. As we sat to catch up, she threw at me what felt like a curveball. "Have you ever thought about capturing your life story in a book?" she asked me candidly.

Caught off guard, I sipped my coffee as I bought time to think through her question for a moment before probing further. "Why do you ask?" To my amazement my friend simply said, "Because your life would instruct those who are just beginning life with nothing and inspire hope for a better life."

I shrugged her off with the promise that I would give it a thought. You see I run a busy medical spa, and have to balance many moving parts of my life. A book was the last thing I would have thought of fitting into my already busy schedule. It felt easier to put off the idea of writing a book and instead focus on balancing my already busy life.

However, the thought of writing a book never died off, as every once in a while it would stalk me like a tidal wave. That week when the push in my spirit was too strong to ignore, I decided to confide in my husband somehow hoping he would talk me out of the idea.

"Honey, I am thinking of writing a book!" I shared casually with him over a phone conversation. I sensed the excitement in his voice when he asked me to tell him more about it. And when I shared some ideas I had mulled over, he responded in a matter of fact way, "I wonder what took you so long to see that."

He went on to relate inspiring scenarios in my life that were exactly what I would want this book to capture; From my speaking engagements in Amway to my involvement in our local church in Ontario. He encouraged me and asked me to seek counsel on how to publish a book from a friend who is an accomplished author. The die was cast.

I got in touch with my author friend and after our meeting I knew there was no turning back. I left the meeting ready and excited to tell my story. A simple story of my ordinary life that demonstrates one can live a full life and if you are audacious enough to chase after your dreams, you will achieve them no matter who you are, where you come from, or what you have gone through in life. Through it all God can carry you from grace to grace.

Like most debut authors, I am filled with excitement and anxiety upon the book's publication. Excitement that the book will inspire and transform someone beyond my wildest dreams, anxiety that I have failed to say anything worth saying. Either way I will take my chances, and hopefully this will stir you to take your chances at your dreams.

Happy reading!

Chapter 1

Your past doesn't determine your future.

You are not a product of your circumstances.
You are a product of your decisions.
– Stephen Covey

I RECALL FEELING THE NEED to work a little harder at everything in life including gaining my dad's attention. This feeling goes back to my childhood days. Ours was a polygamous family and so not only was my dad's time, attention and energy split between his two wives but in addition to that, we had to share him with his political allies. My mum is the second wife; funny thing is that she and my step mother got married almost at the same time.

Dad's political star shone especially during former president Moi's regime. Consequently, he was away from home most of the time. Possibly that or the fact that I spent a lot of time with mum that naturally we became quite close. Being the first born and a girl, I took up a lot of responsibilities at an early age; assisting mum with feeding my siblings and ensuring they were ready for school.

This responsibility never left me and unbelievably to date, I always feel as if my siblings are my children despite the slight age gap between us. Like mother hen, their pain becomes my pain, whatever concerns them concerns me too; irrespective of us all being adults. I believe this is the case with many first-borns. Possibly, the first–born curse or blessing depending on how you choose to see it.

My dad's involvement in politics came with its perks. At the time, we were the only homestead that owned a car and a TV set amongst other things that were rare luxuries in our village in Nanyuki town, Laikipia County. We were the envy of the village although for a short period. Dad ended up losing a colossal amount of money in a business deal that went sour. This spiraled into a court case. We ended up bankrupt and auctioneers came knocking.

The realization that life changes often spontaneously and without warning, hit home really hard. I particularly remember catching a glimpse of mum crying hysterically as the auctioneers emptied the house of all items we considered valuable including a new cooker that she had saved for so long to acquire and had barely used it.

Nothing breaks your heart like watching your mother in pain and feeling utterly helpless to alleviate her suffering. I am emotional even as I recall this. The feeling of utter helplessness being a child and unable to do anything to ease the pain your mother is going through is just heartbreaking. I cried and wondered how cold and cruel life could be. Mothers are truly angels with given special grace. There are huge sacrifices that they make and endure painful ordeals for the families, most of which go unrecognised.

I still had to go to school the next day and to add to the embarrassment of losing our property, I also had to deal with the curious stares, whispers and sympathy from students most of whom came from my village.

The news of the auction had spread in the village like a wild fire. What ensued in school was the raucous laughter and teasing from my schoolmates as I walked past them. I have never been one to like pity from others. It makes you feel helpless, like you are doomed to that situation for good. Although in my young mind I had no answers, I knew my family had suffered a pitfall but somehow I had the conviction our fortunes would change one day but I didn't know how. This was an extremely painful and humiliating experience. Convinced that I couldn't take the ridicule anymore I persuaded dad to put an end to my agony by transferring me to another school. To my delight, he agreed.

My transfer from a school in my neighbourhood to one that was far from home was a much welcomed move. However this meant waking up at 5:00 am to be in school by 7:30 am. I believe this was when I learned that life is not always going to be rosy and there will be tough moments but even then you need to build your enduring spirit. With mum having lost her cooker to the auction, I had to get up earlier than usual to start the fire and make my morning tea before walking to school, 10 kilometres away. Those were not the days of Uber or children being dropped off to school by their parents. Even the idea of a school owning a bus that would ferry pupils to and from school like today where this is a norm, was a far-fetched idea. How times have changed!

I had to endure the biting cold as I walked past the thick bushes at 6:00am daily not to mention carrying a heavy load of books, lunch and drinking water, as these were not provided by the school. Even then, I was happy as there weren't any students at the new school who were aware of my family situation.

But just when you think you have escaped one trouble, you come face to face with another. Such is life. At the new school, I had to deal with bullying from some of the older students. This time there was no running away from trouble and I couldn't bear to burden my dad with yet another transfer. Sadly to date bullying remains a huge problem in many schools, not just in Kenya but worldwide. Bullying takes not just the physical form but also nonphysical forms including cyber bullying which has become so rampant and unfortunately in some incidences it has resulted to suicide. It calls for a combined effort between the school administration, the student body and parents to fight this vice.

Looking back, I have since learnt that life is filled with challenges. It doesn't matter who you are, no one goes through life unscathed. As long as life continues there will be a set of new challenges and the idea of waiting until everything is perfect for you to enjoy life is quite the lie. Perfection doesn't exist either, it only does in our heads because we make it up.

Think about it, many people seem to be waiting for the struggles of life to end. We work hard with the goal of making enough money hoping that one day we will just sit back and do nothing other than enjoy it all. How wrong of us!

As you grow older, you learn that as soon as you make this money, you are going to need to work even harder to maintain it. The struggle doesn't end; instead you get a new set of struggles.

What really helps is acknowledging that life will always present you with one set of struggle after another and rather than getting surprised and frustrated at it, you choose to enjoy the moment regardless. American entrepreneur, author and motivation speaker Jim Rohn couldn't have said it better, "Do not wish it was easier, wish you were better. Do not wish for fewer problems, wish for more skills." This is an important lesson for both children and adults. If there was a time when parents ought to equip their children with life skills it is now. Many children of today's generation of instant gratification lack basic skills to cope with the turbulences of life. Yet in a constantly changing environment, having life skills is an essential part of growing up. For instance when a child runs to a parent for answers are you quick to provide these? The best thing you can do is to strive to first listen and gauge the child's views and thought processes rather than being quick to provide a solution. This is the best way to equip children with problem-solving skills because you won't always be there and it is important that children learn to think for themselves, weigh their choices in life and make good decisions.

Of course as a young girl in primary school, I didn't know of this wisdom but I stayed put and toughened it up. I was just settling into the new school when I got into an accident during a physical education (P.E) class and broke my leg. For two months, I had to be off school to nurse the fracture. This affected me academically; not only was I dealing with my family's financial issues but I was also nursing a broken leg.

Two years later, I was happy to join high school as a boarder. It was here that the dream of getting out of the village was birthed. With the financial troubles in my family, I had a strong conviction that I needed to work extra hard.

I did not want to ever feel inadequate. Neither was I keen to be financially dependent on anyone, if anything I wanted to change the financial situation of my family. But to do this, I needed to get away.

Perhaps it was the burden of being a first born that made me feel it was my responsibility to change the financial circumstances in my family. No one ever verbalised it, I just felt naturally my individual success would impact on my entire family. I recall one time dad paid me a visit at school. At the time, mum had been unwell for sometime warranting an admission at the hospital.

Later, in a conversation with one of his friends, I overheard him disclose that mum's hospital bill was getting out of hand. His best efforts to raise funds and clear the bill were not enough. He felt utterly helpless and was desperate.

But even the worst situations have a silver lining. In mum's case it was my aunt who lived in the UK that became the saving grace of the family. Her financial assistance enabled dad to clear the hospital bill; a gesture that build a deep conviction in me that I needed to get away from the village, go out into the world and take my chances at succeeding in life.

My aunt became my role model and the more I looked up to her the more my dreams felt plausible. I dreamt of a time when I would be able to support my family financially. At the age of 18, I left for the UK. This, I believe was the beginning of my journey to greatness.

Being away from the familiar comfort of my parents was liberating yet at the same time scary. It built my resilience and competence in life as I had to learn how best to survive and fit in a new foreign environment and negotiate my way around. This is what got me out of my shell and shaped me to a young confident woman, able to adapt to different situations.

Meeting new people, experiencing different cultures, trying new foods, learning a new language, seeing new sights are some of the benefits of traveling. But in addition to that travelling broadens your mind and presents you with a myriad of opportunities that you hadn't seen or even dreamt of before.

One of the greatest pieces of advice I would give to anyone and especially any young person is to look out for opportunities to travel. This is because when you are young, chances are high that you haven't really settled on what path to follow. You are still growing and experimenting which is a great stage of life to be at and to see what the world has to offer.

When you travel, you truly understand that the world is your oyster. Since my first travel to the UK at the age of 18, I have had the privilege of travelling across the world numerous times and interacted with people from all walks of life. Whenever people learn of my humble beginning, they get astonished. I am a testament that one's past is not a determinant of what their future holds. Now older and wiser, I know many more women ought to hoot about their life's accomplishments because these go a long way in inspiring others. My encouragement to women is to document their successes difficult as it may seem and I know this too well, because many of us are brought up believing that we should let our accomplishments speak for themselves, rather than us talking about what we have achieved. It took me courage to overcome this and author this book.

I believe young women, just like in my case, can learn to dream big through seeing the successes of other women who have gone ahead of them in life. We therefore need to ask ourselves how will the youth learn if we shy off from parading the hurdles we have overcome and the successes we have attained? I know what you are thinking; that this is pride, it isn't. When you realize how the life of one young person can change forever just because you chose to share your story then you know it is worth it. I think of my two beautiful daughters and the opportunities they have today. I not only pray but I am also very intentional about exposing them to the world, to the great feats of those who have gone ahead of them. My encouragement to them is to be the very best versions of themselves, whatever that may be.

With friends before leaving for the UK

Chapter 2

Faith in God is everything.

When I let go of what I am, I become what I might be.
-Lao Tzu

WITHOUT GOD AND HIS POWERFUL word therein the bible, I truly don't know what would be of my life. I remain indebted to my mum for laying a Christian foundation at a very early age. This has shaped me to whom I am today. My journey in faith goes back to my childhood days where I was part of both the church and school choir. It was during this period when I gave my life to Christ at the age of 14. Although my mum was very happy and proud of me, she was not too sure if I truly understood what getting saved meant.

I must admit she was right since it only took a short time for me to be drawn back to the worldly delights. Dancing and entertainment were the life of high school and dancing to the beat of Madonna, who was such a hit at the time, was the highlight of my day. A part of me was afraid that being a Christian would mean I had to choose between having a life and settling for a boring one.

My attempts to try and be a Christian while at the same time have a life meant that I keep dancing to Madonna even as I attended the Christian Union.

At the time I did not realise that my faith ought to be more about my relationship with God rather than following a set of Dos and Don'ts. And so I interpreted my slightest indication of a struggle in faith to mean I was falling off the Christian bandwagon. This was often followed by guilt, fear and shame. How exhausting! I have since learnt that God is more interested in the state of my heart. As I establish a relationship with him, have a deeper love and walk with him, I get convicted of sin and the things that break His heart. Gradually I find that my desires change and notice that naturally I start detaching from the things I used to do that break His heart. Don't get me wrong I am not perfect and God knows that and He doesn't expect me or any other person to be perfect. He knows I still sin, but even as He convicts me of my sin, His love for me remains unconditional. What a loving father!

By the time I was heading to college in the UK, I had fallen in love with a boy from my village. The thought of being away from him was so unbearable that I had some reservations about leaving him behind. I was afraid that if I left, I would lock myself out from the possibility of getting married to him or anyone else for that matter.

At the time this felt like the most difficult decision I would make in life, little did I know that life is a series of making one decision after another. Nevertheless, I had to be true to myself and the promise I had made to myself years ago that I would take up the slightest opportunity I got to get out of the village. The chance had presented itself and I needed to grab it and have faith that this new path was worth the sacrifice and that it would pay off someday.

My parents saw me off at the airport with the reassurance that I was always welcome to return home if life abroad proved not to be what I expected it to be. This was going to be my very first experience on an airplane.

My excitement was also tinged with fear that the plane might crash. After several hours of travel, nervous yet at the same time excited to see the world, I finally got to the UK. It was everything that I had imagined and dreamt of-at least at the first glance. A clean yet very organized mess would be my best description of it; nothing close to the image of a bed of roses that is sometimes portrayed in media. Life wasn't easy either and despite my parents' support, I still had to work in between studies just to make ends meet.

At some point, life felt more difficult abroad. Unlike at home where I could go to my parents whenever I wanted something, I now had to work for anything I needed. Life demanded that I make decisions which at the age of 18 years seemed difficult. Between obeying instructions from your parents and teachers who decide basic things including what to eat, where to eat and when to eat, many children never learn to make any decisions for themselves before the age of 18.

And so when I was required to be responsible for my life, it felt as if I had been thrown in the deep end and forced to swim with the sharks. It helped that I was able to make friends easily; one of whom eventually became my roommate in a shared apartment that we got together. She would over time introduce me to her circle of friends. And it was at around this time that I met Martin.

Like a house on fire, Martin and I hit it off immediately. There is something about connecting with a fellow citizen while in a foreign land. It doesn't matter if the two of you are strangers. That shared commonality is enough to get you going. Shortly thereafter, I got a referral from a Kenyan lady to try out a nursing auxiliary course that would give me the credits needed to join nursing school and thereby increase my odds of getting a better paying job.

Things were beginning to settle in but as much as I was starting to get comfortable in the new environment, I never once forgot what took me away from home as well as my family back at home. This always kept me focused.

At around the same time, my brother was also joining university in Kenya and I had to see how best to support him financially. Although his tuition fee was already catered for, I wanted to ensure he had money for his toiletries and a little pocket money. The first born streak in me couldn't help but nurture and lead my younger siblings. In his book *The Birth Order Book of Love*, William Cane says your personality is directly related to how you interact with others. I find that this is very true of me and not just with my siblings. Many times I take charge of things so naturally so much so that many of those who know me will describe me as ambitious, a leader and generous.

I truly believe the best way to live out one's faith is to selflessly give. Giving is not always financial; It could be one's time and talents. The concept of giving is best articulated in Ecclesiastics 7:1 that says a good name is more precious than fine perfume. Jesus remains the best role model we all can learn from as His good name and memory has lasted for centuries and from generation to generation.

Throughout my life in faith there have been times when things have gotten out of order and life has tried to bend me in the wrong direction. But it is at those times that I remain even more determined to depend on God.

At the Age of 21, I returned to Kenya for a short visit and stayed on for a couple of weeks. My return had mixed feelings and experiences because I didn't gel well with my old friends. In the three years I was away, I had become outspoken and that brought some sour moments with some of my family members. My dad in particularly picked a bone with me because he misconstrued my being outspoken for rudeness.

The truth is I was growing up, changing and learning to define life for myself. I truly believe one can't gain new experiences in life and remain the same. And there is nothing wrong with change, if anything change is the only constant factor in life. However, many times people are so afraid to change but if anything we should be more afraid of remaining the same because it means we are not growing. Change is good especially when it causes personal growth. To be honest, If you are to live out your full potential, you are definitely going to change, try out new things, embrace new ideas and new experiences. It is all part of growing up.

Even then, whenever there was a tiff between dad and I, I still leaned on God for wisdom on how best to handle myself while around my family until my return to the UK.

Chapter 3

Just because you love someone doesn't mean they won't hurt you.

Prosperity makes friends. Adversity tries them.
– Publilius Syrus

IN 1995, I RETURNED TO the UK after my short visit to Kenya. Four months later and to my great surprise I discovered I was pregnant. My first reaction was that I had let down my parents. Thoughts of the sacrifices they had made for me to get a decent education abroad only for me to get pregnant plagued my mind.

Fear, confusion, disappointment and uncertainty consumed me. I was afraid that this meant I had sabotaged my chances of being successful in life. It didn't matter how close I was to my parents and especially my mum, I still wondered how they would react to this new realization. They had taught me better and emphasized that premarital sex was against the Christian values and beliefs they had instilled in me.

First I had to break the news to my boyfriend Martin. I must admit I was pleasantly surprised at how excited he was at the news. His constant reassurance of his love and support made it easier for me to eventually break the news to my parents when the time came.

Nonetheless, fear still crept back in me. Both Martin and I were young and I had not envisaged myself raising a child at the age of 21. If anything I still felt I was a child and needed my mum. As cliché as this may sound, truly nothing makes you appreciate your mother more than the realization that you are soon going to be a mother. You start appreciating your mother for everything she is. You recognize that she not only gave you life but shaped you into the woman you are today and that alone leaves you at a loss on how best to show your gratitude to her. You reflect on all the love and sacrifices she has made for you and recall all the trouble you've put her through especially in your younger days and can't help but cry at how foolish you have been. Truly, there is no greater responsibility in life than the one bestowed upon someone with the decision to raise a child.

Apart from worrying about my parent's reaction, being a first born, I was also afraid how my actions would be interpreted by siblings and even influence them. There is often a huge sense of unspoken responsibility that is pegged on first borns, and you just have to be one to know it. Younger siblings follow your footsteps and even though they may not always come to you for guidance, they silently observe what you do and in many ways they begin to imitate you.

As a first born you therefore grow up conditioned to want to do things right always. You feel like there is no room for mistakes, because there are so many expectations from you that you just can't afford to mess up. Many times you feel the pressure of the great expectations placed on you not just by your family but also by the society. You learn to take charge, to give instructions, to become self-sufficient because you have to look after younger siblings even though you have no older sibling to look out for you.

Many first borns talk about how they had to baby sit their younger siblings, forgo something so that the younger siblings could have it, mediate rivalry among siblings, stand-up for their siblings against their parents as well as bullies from school or in the neighbourhood. In addition, many can relate to their childhood experience of getting a thorough beating from their parents because of something wrong one of their younger siblings did. You somehow had to take the fall for it because even though you are a kid yourself you should know better and guide your younger siblings.

This reminds me of an incident as a teenager when I was left to care for my younger siblings while my parents went to work. That day my parents were a little late than usual to return home. We had eaten dinner when my siblings began running around playing.

That evening, we were also in the company of a young girl who mum had temporarily taken in. She had volunteered to help with cleaning the dishes since I had done the cooking. She had just taken a pot of hot water from the fire and placed it on the ground to cool off when my younger sister Edith came running and accidentally fell right in it.

Her piercing screams rented the air alerting the attention of all and sundry. As the eldest child I needed to quickly take action only that I couldn't think. I found myself scared to death and screaming for help from the neighbours who gathered in no time. When we finally assisted Edith to get out of the pot and take off the clothes she was wearing, her top came off but the bottom was stuck to her skin. Horrified, my other siblings started screaming and crying at the same time.

Edith needed to be rushed to hospital but those were not the days of mobile phones and there was no way of alerting my parents what had transpired. Together with a neighbour, we assisted Edith to walk as we headed towards the main road in search of public transport to take her to the nearest hospital. Just as we were approaching the edge of the dusty road that led to the main highway, we were met by the sight of someone flashing their headlights. Thank God it was my parents driving home.

Distressed, mum spotted us and hurriedly got out of the car and walked quickly towards us with the look of worry written all over her face. She bombarded us with all sorts of questions directed at me. I remember feeling helpless and guilty despite knowing that I wasn't to blame for it. I sobbed amidst narrating to her the events that had taken place leading to the accident. I hoped my sister would be okay but at the same time I hated being the one who was left in charge only for this to happen.

I knew I wasn't going to get off the hook on this incident anytime soon. Dad was furious although he comforted and reassured me that my sister was going to be okay.

That night and for many nights that followed, Edith and mum didn't leave the hospital. Yet again I took up the role of a caregiver to my other siblings. When I think of the role of first borns I can't help but conclude that no wonder in biblical days, first borns got a double portion of every inheritance. They carry such a huge burden.

Although Edith eventually got better she still has visible scars on her legs that are a reminder of that incident. Many times when I see the marks on her legs I can't help but recall that day and somehow feel responsible for it.

As a first born, it does not matter how far away you are from home, or how independent your life is or even how old you are, somehow even as you make decisions about your life, you hope the outcome will be taken in positive light especially by those who look up to you.

After gathering enough courage I finally broke the news of my pregnancy to mum over a phone conversation. I could still sense a strain of disappointment from her voice despite her encouraging me and pledging her support to Martin and I as long we were both in it.

However, there were still members of my family who disapproved of Martin. And some of his family members felt the same about me. They were worried that Martin was young and raising a child would be a huge responsibility for him to take up, one that could slow down his ambitions in life. There is an old fashioned myth that being a parent automatically means that you can't have a successful career and especially if you are young. Whereas I admit that parenting and career can be challenging and especially more so for women, even so, it is do-able.

Martin and I realised we could only count on ourselves and so we had to toughen up as the journey wasn't easy. For instance, at some point we were kicked out of the UK apartment that we were living in, at a time when I was heavily pregnant. The apartments belonged to my aunt and although I was paying rent at the time, she still felt betrayed that Martin and I had moved in together under the disguise that we were roommates and wanted to share the cost of rent.

The truth is we wanted to be together, like any couple in love would. It didn't make sense for us to live apart considering I was pregnant and we had plans of raising a family together. Fortunately, we were able to get another apartment albeit smaller, where our first child Sandra, was born.

Martin and I relied on each other and God. We were very hopeful that this was enough to get us by and it didn't matter what other people or close family members were saying behind our backs.

I think this was the one time I realized that those you sometimes love the most, are the very ones who will hurt and disappoint you the most. That includes not just friends but close family too. However, you have a choice either to be angry and bitter about it for the rest of your life, or to feel the anger at least for some time, and then decide to forgive, move on and even extend grace to them despite your disappointments.

When you learn that we all are human, deeply flawed and prone to hurt others even those we love, then you learn to forgive easily. In my experience, I have learnt life gets much easier when you learn to accept all the apologies that you never get. People will sometimes hurt you and still carry on like they haven't done anything to you. You have a choice to accept every situation you face, good or bad as a lesson in life..

I used to hoard my forgiveness until I realized unforgiveness creates a roller coaster of negative emotions. I could also reference the bible verse that encourages people to forgive each other for them to expect forgiveness from God.

But let no one lie that forgiveness is easy, it isn't but it's necessary. Sometimes we need to forgive people due to their ignorance or weaknesses but not necessarily because we are weaker.

And you don't even realise how hard forgiveness is until you have to forgive a close friend or family member. It almost feels like you would rather die than forgive. You analyse the situation by saying if the person really cared about you, they would never do what they did. The more you think and analyse the situation, the deeper your anger sits in.

I didn't think much of any of these until one day when I was driving home from work. I began playing a very upsetting scene in my head of something my dad had done to me and all of a sudden I was going through a roller coaster of emotions, my mood changed and the road seemed blurry. I was seething in anger. I almost crashed yet I couldn't stop my mind from playing the scene over and over again. I pulled up by the roadside, parked the car and then broke down. I must have been very upset because I cried for a long time trying to calm myself down, after which I said a prayer and somehow I was able to compose myself and drive home.

That was when I realized that my unforgiveness was getting out of control and if I wasn't careful then it would have sank into depression. From that day on I resolved that it didn't matter what anyone did to me I was always going to forgive not because I take hurt lightly but for my own good. Keeping a grudge is a perfect waste of your happiness, and holding onto one is like allowing unwanted company to come and live rent-free in your head.

When you choose to forgive someone whether or not they apologized to you, you are freeing yourself of the burden of being a victim forever. However, this is only possible through faith because humanly speaking being resentful is much easier than forgiving.

It is true of the saying that nothing is permanent in life, not even one's troubles. At some point our fortunes changed and through God's blessings my husband and I were able to move into a bigger apartment. For once we both felt we were living like a family should, but this did not come without its new set of challenges. Due to our lack of experience in parenthood we had numerous conflicts on who was to take care of our baby, when and how.

We longed for parental guidance and advice at this critical time and with both families far away the situation was made more complicated.

In one instance, I went to work on night shift and left my husband with the baby. When I got back home in the morning I was met by the sight of our baby who had thrown up and was crying uncontrollably. Martin had dozed off, oblivious of the cries from the baby. Frustrated, I took the baby, cleaned her up, drove off and switched off my phone. I was angry at Martin. It was only much later that I called a friend, told her where I was and what had transpired. She tried to convince me to return home but I was adamant.

Now In retrospect, I acknowledge that nothing truly prepares you enough for parenting. There are days you wake up to the screams of your little one in the middle of the night an hour or so into your slumber and yet you still need to be up quite early. In such moments you are torn between ignoring the baby so that you can catch a few winks, and the guilt of your child's panic-stricken cries.

In attempts to uphold a super-parent status, many parents do not openly share their challenges with others. We pretend that parenting is all joy and there is never any pain or challenge because often we are afraid of judgment and criticism from others.

We want the world to think that we have it all together, and so we put on a mask and smile even when all we want to do is scream. Yet by failing to openly admit and even share some of our painful experiences in parenting, we end up alienating ourselves from others. And many times this alienation causes us to believe falsely that we are the only ones feeling this way. How unfortunate!

My parenting experience has been a mix of joy and pain, yet very fulfilling. Although parenting is one of the most rewarding things in life, it will often leave you overstretched and stressed out. You learn to become the best juggler; handling family, work, marriage, friendships, money and whatever else life throws at you. And there is no manual for it; you just figure it out as you go but it really helps to have a great support system around you.

In my parenting experience what has kept me going over the years is acknowledging that each stage of life is seasonal. When children are young, they will need more of your time and energy hence consume your every moment awake but as they get older they become more independent and need less of you, hence freeing your time a bit more.

Pregnant with Sandra

Thanks to God's grace, Martin and I survived the hard work of raising Sandra in the first year, where it felt as if we were literally walking on eggshells. And on her second birthday, Martin proposed to me and we rolled out plans to solemnize our union.

Being the first among my close circle of friends to get a baby, Sandra got a chance to be raised by a bunch of young adults, full of life and love. They are a great reminder that it takes a village to raise a child.

I am thankful too that I had very supportive friends, such as my friend Catherine who has always been a second mother to Sandra. In addition,

God also sent me a friend by the name Saiqa, whose family is from Pakistan although she was born and raised in the UK. Saiqa's family fell in love with Sandra and took up the role of grandparents, aunties and uncles. Severally they watched Sandra as Martin and I were at work because at the time we couldn't afford to hire a nanny although we needed one badly. On days when I was exhausted from sleepless nights coupled with many hours of working, Saiqa's family would watch Sandra and allow me to take a nap and rest without worrying about my baby's whereabouts.

They would also offer to babysit her and allow Martin and I to go on a date and spend some alone, quality time together. I am so grateful to them because they contributed in a huge way to the success of our relationship and parenting experience. We all could do with such loving people in our lives. They went ahead to become part of my wedding when I finally got married to Martin. I recall as a young bride, Saiqa's mother took time to come into my house and teach me how to prepare delicious meals for my husband. She was patient with me and taught me how to cook *pilau*, a rice delicacy. She recognized as a young bride I needed some guidance and being miles away from home and from my mother, she stepped into her shoes. Whenever I think of how Saiqa's family has contributed to my life and that of my family, my heart beams with joy.

Every year, for the last 21 years, I have watched as Saiqa takes her time as well as spend her money gifting Sandra on her birthday as an expression of her love. It is amazing that she considers Sandra her daughter and all these years on her love for my daughter is still outpouring. The two of them share a beautiful bond and I am so glad that Sandra has such a great example to learn from about what it means to love people regardless of their tribe, age, race or religion. This is especially important at this time when the world has become hateful and intolerant of others because of their religious, tribal and racial difference.

Rather than embrace and love each other, many of us have used the opportunity to show supremacy and treat each other with suspicion and spew so much hate around. How sad! I think we all need to do a lot of soul searching and be intentional about accommodating differences, being open to learning from each other's differences and just loving on each. If we choose to see people for who they are rather than their religion, tribe or race then the world will definitely be a much better place to live in. The world could do with some more love if you ask me.

I shudder to think what beautiful love I would be denying Sandra from experiencing, if I shut out Saiqa from her life on the basis that she is a Muslim whereas we are Christians. True love transcends race, tribe, religion and cultural differences.

Saiqa's family serve as a great example of how God can use people irrespective of race, religion or status quo to bless you. Even the bible says in 1st john 4 20-21; whoever claims to love God yet hates a brother or sister is a liar. For whoever does not love their brother and sister, whom they have seen, cannot love God, whom they have not seen. And He has given us this command: Anyone who loves God must also love their brother and sister. To date I consider Saiqa's family, my family.

Celebrating my 19th birthday with Catherine

Chapter 4

Life without love is useless.

Without friends, no one would choose to live, though he had all other goods.
– Aristotle

AT 43, I CAN CONFIDENTLY say without love life is not worth living. The need to belong, to love, to be affectionate is an inherent need that exists, and is ingrained within us from the point we gain consciousness. Love is the very foundation of our existence; its soothing attributes topping the list of the reasons why.

All of us have the desire to love and be loved; the kind of love that never ends, this is just part of us being human whether we like it or not. However betrayal, hurt, abandonment and disappointment makes us freeze and fight that unquenchable hope of true love. We suppress it down and choose to substitute it with love of material things and any pleasures that make us feel good, not knowing that through all this we're shutting down our hearts to the possibility of real love.

For instance if a stranger makes small talk with you in a kind or warm way chances are that you will respond to them much more easier however unimportant the conversation may be about, than if they were rude or harsh to you.

I would rather have love and miss out on everything else in life. When you know that you're loved and that you love back, it is truly magical. Regardless of your relationship status, loving the people around you is the most important thing that one can do. I have since learnt to appreciate love at different levels in its purest form and never to take it for granted. The words "I love you" carry so much weight and this can be demonstrated not just by words but by actions too. For instance, you can bring healing to someone who is unwell by your presence and show of genuine care, which is equated to love.

My life has been one huge adventure lived with a variety of experiences and a range of emotions but love makes it a beautiful life. Some of the best expressions of love for me were when my husband and I took our wedding vows and promised to love each other till death do us part. I thought I had experienced true love when I got married and true to my words I was really happy that explains why I'm still married today.

But even so when I got into my marriage I realised my husband was human and capable of doing things that sometimes left me feeling unloved. I was still searching for answers as to how a person can love you and yet still hurt you when I came across the story of the life of Jesus and had a light bulb moment.

I realised that loving people means sometimes you will disappoint them. Think about this; Jesus with all the selfless and unconditional love he freely gives to us, yet we all have had thoughts of feeling unloved, disappointed and even unhappy with Him from time to time. How much more do you expect from man?

It dawned on me that the only one who can truly love me is God because he doesn't need anything from me, if anything I need Him. This truth liberated me to live a full life. I didn't have to just trudge through life to meet my responsibilities and expect someone else to make me happy. I had the freedom of choosing to enjoy God's gifts every day by just accepting and acknowledging that only He is in control of my life and that He orders my steps if I let Him and live according to His will.

Then there was the birth of our children; a time when Martin and I expressed our love and support to bring up our children the best way we knew how. On September 24, 2005, my husband, Sandra and I went to the grocery store to do our usual weekly shopping. I was eight month's pregnant at the time with our second baby Maxine.

We had just completed our shopping when I started experiencing sharp labour pains. Martin quickly rushed me to the hospital. I remember things were happening so fast and before I knew it, I was being wheeled off to theatre. The doctors needed to do an emergency Caesarian section to save my baby's life. Amidst the panic and confusion, Martin and I authorised it.

When Maxine was born she was so tiny. I had read so much about premature births that I decided to hold her close to my chest day and night. No one else except me and Martin held her during this period. I had done so for two days and on the third night, after my husband had left the hospital, the nurses insisted on taking Maxine to her nursery to sleep so that I too could get some rest. But I would hear none of it. Through the assistance of the doctors, the nurses finally managed to get the baby off me.

Desperate, I got out bed and started praying, bargaining with God that if He let my baby and I go home in the next few days, I would be the best mother any child could ask for. So loud and hysterical was I that I attracted the attention of the nurses. Their pleas for me to get back to bed and get some rest fell on deaf ears. I wouldn't talk to the nurses.

Confused at how best to handle me, they alerted my husband that he was needed at the hospital the following day as early as possible. In the meantime, they had brought in a psychiatrist to evaluate my state of mind.

So dramatic was I that the more the psychiatrist asked me myriad of questions the more hysterical I became. I went on and on praying for hours, loudly. By the time I was done, I had faith beyond any shadow of doubt that my daughter and I were going to be okay and would go home in couple of days. For the very first time I experienced what the bible terms as peace that surpasses human understanding. No doubt there is power in prayer; God is able to do more than we can ask or even imagine.

By the time my husband got to the hospital in the morning, I had showered and dressed up. I recall the look of confusion on his face. He couldn't understand the emergency he had been alerted about because everything seemed calm. And neither could the doctors and nurses believe I was the same person they had dealt with the previous night. A mother's love for her child is like nothing else in the world. It can make you do crazy things.

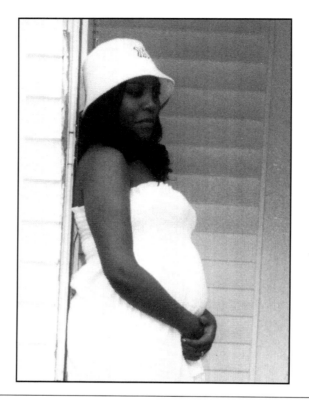

Expectant with Maxine

In a week's time, Maxine and I were discharged from hospital with a clean bill of health. Today Maxine is a strong, bubbly beautiful girl that no one would believe came into the world in such a dramatic manner.

The kind of love that I still enjoy with my 70-year-old dad and 60-year-old mum is blissful as they still see me as their little girl. This love is one that has morphed with age; so much so that now I can't imagine life without my mum which wasn't the case in my teenage.

It is amazing how our relationship with our parents tend to spill over and affect the relationships we have as adults. Neil Strauss says in his book, *The Truth: An uncomfortable Book about Relationship,* that romantic relationships in adulthood are shaped by our experiences as children. "Our first experience with love is with our parents," he says and add that this sets the template for how we see love and what we want out of love.

Admittedly, in my case my relationship with my dad has had its share of ups and downs, nevertheless I loved and still love him dearly. However, this affected my relationships and made it difficult for me to open up to any man during my dating years. It has taken a lot of patience, trust and love for me and my husband to get through this.

When it comes to my siblings, the kind of bond we share is very strong. In many instances, siblings tend to become our first friends. We confide in them, collaborate and even conspire against our parents with them.

In many ways our siblings become our cheerleaders, inspiration and role models. They teach us the true value of friendships as well as conflict resolution way before we can step out into the world. Although this is true of me and all my siblings, I must admit I share an even closer bond with my immediate sibling and I see a lot of us in my two children and the close bond they share.

But being a first born I have always felt that all my siblings are my responsibility, much like my children are. When they hurt I hurt, when they succeed in life, I feel successful too and beam with joy. I believe there is nothing that can come between us regardless of the challenges or conflicts that we often have.

Somehow at the end of the day, we know that we will always have each other's back no matter what. I pray about it too because a life without love is useless. No amount of money can buy genuine love.

Wedding bells

Chapter 5

Build a wall of beautiful memories.

The best part of a road trip isn't arriving at your destination.
It's all the wild stuff that happens along the way.
— Emma Chase

IN A FAST-MOVING WORLD, IT often feels like there isn't time to pause and capture beautiful moments. We seem to always be in a rush to get to somewhere and do something important. But I have learnt that even so it is equally important on a daily basis to slow down and enjoy what is happening in the present. Many of us are socialized to believe that a crazy-busy life is a productive and good life. We are pulled daily into different directions, by a never-ending to do list. This is unhealthy.

You have to be intentional about finding some time to rest and enjoy life because this is what you miss out on when you have a very busy life. This reminds me of Elizabeth Gilbert's *Eat, Pray, Love* memoir where she writes about a friend who whenever she sees a beautiful place she exclaims in near panic, "It is so beautiful here I want to come back here someday!" Gilbert writes," It takes all my persuasive power to try and convince my friend that she is already here.''

Some of the practical ways I have adopted over the years in my bid to try as much as possible to live in the present and which you can borrow include:

Deliberately choosing to single task. Whereas I acknowledge that deadlines are always beckoning and it feels like everyone advocates for multi-tasking and sometimes it is unavoidable, once in a while I try to single task by scheduling one task at a time. In my line of work, appointments and time-keeping is very important. Single-tasking can actually help you achieve much as research has shown that by actually focusing on one task at a time, you become competent and achieve much.

Enjoying a few minutes of total silence. Taking time especially over the weekend to sit at a park, a garden at the restaurant or in-doors and enjoy a few minutes of silence alone, away from everyone, noise or music. This helps me reconnect with my thoughts and simply enjoy my own company. I also enjoy taking some time to pamper myself in the spa and relax. No wonder I run a spa!

Savouring a meal uninterrupted. Sitting and eating undisturbed for at least one meal a day. Whether I am having a cup coffee, lunch or diner I choose the meal of the day that I eat slowly, taking my time to savour every bite rather than eating as I work or while on the commute.

Setting time aside to pray and meditate. My faith is a core part of my life and nothing aligns my day better than prayer. And so I try to set the tone for my day early in the morning by reading my bible, praying and reflecting on the word of God before heading out to face the day.

Focus on the person you are talking to. It is very easy to be in the midst of a conversation with someone but you are totally zoned out. Sometimes when you pay close attention to someone you are able to hear even that which they are not telling you about. You can do this by making eye contact and then you will be able to read their body language as well.

Taking time off and going on vacation. Many people are afraid to take time off their business or work to go on holiday and when they do, they spend as much time working just as they do in the office. My vacations are a time to relax and rest, and so work and laptop are off limits. Do not allow excuses to stop you from taking time to rest such as you are afraid of the backlog, no one else can do the job while you are away or that you are afraid of being replaced at your job. You will be surprised just how a few days off work can get you relaxed and re-energized.

Spending time with the family, taking a walk in the park, catching up over coffee, going hiking, taking time to connect with employees, is very vital but is often overlooked by the hectic routines that have taken up most of our lives. These seemingly little things in life are actually the big and important things that I have come to cherish the most.

In my case, I have a day each week that I choose not to schedule any meetings but use this time to breath, relax, reflect or call up an old friend just to catch up. This has a refreshing effect and puts me in balance with everything else that is happening around me.

I love it when my children remind me of the holiday memories they enjoyed most or when my husband reminds me of our expeditions during our dating years, or when a friend reminds me of a fun and relaxing weekend we spent time together. These memorable experiences always give me hope and a place to draw inspiration and strength when I feel depleted. After all what is the point of working so hard and barely having time to enjoy the fruits of your labour?

The bible articulates this in Ecclesiastes 3:1-4 "To everything there is a season and a time to every purpose under the heaven. A time to be born and a time to die; a time to plant and a time to pluck up that which is planted; A time to kill and a time to heal; a time to break down and a time to build up; A time to weep and a time to laugh; a time to mourn and a time to dance." Therefore take time to breath and enjoy today.

Not many people are able to live in the present moment. Some mourn their pasts, its faults and blunders, its aches and pains despite it being beyond their control because it is already gone. The truth is nothing can bring back yesterday. On the other hand others worry about their future, its promises and hopes, its burdens and worries, yet tomorrow isn't guaranteed. However this does not mean that you shouldn't think about the future and even plan for it. But as you do so, don't let it consume you. Remember it is not so much how many years you live but how much life is in your years.

I'm glad I captured most of the memories I had in my mid-twenties and thirties and can now recall them and feel replenished. This is especially important to me now, having left my family in Canada two years ago to return to Kenya and setup my business. It is still tough to date as I often miss them terribly but I always draw strength from my memories file every night before I go to sleep.

Call me old fashion if you like, but even in this era of digital technology, once a while I still enjoy a good printed out photograph rather than a digital one. With this I can frame it and hang it on my wall so that I admire the photo daily and enjoy the memory.

First family vacation

Chapter 6

Giving is one of the most vital things in life.

No person was ever honoured for what he received. Honour has been the reward for what he gave.
– Calvin Coolidge

I TRULY BELIEVE GIVING IS one of the most vital things in life. There is a quote by American actress, producer and director Goldie Hawn that says, giving back is as good for you as it is for those you are helping, because it gives you purpose. When you have a purpose-driven life, you're a happier person. And by giving I don't just mean financially, it could be your time, your experience or your emotional support. There is so much joy derived in giving and the bible supports this in Acts 20: 35, "it is more blessed to give than to receive."

However, naturally we prefer to receive than to give. Giving in many instances does not always feel great. In fact it can make you feel used and taken advantage of. As much as giving is a blessing there is need to have a healthy balance. I learnt to do this by identifying and giving to a cause I believe in, giving into areas where my skills can be utilized, being a proactive and not just a reactive giver as well as refusing to give out of guilt.

I remember in my twenties I always thought my happiness was dependent on receiving. I thought as long as my husband fulfilled all my emotional, financial and physical needs I would be happy. I was greatly disappointed more so because as a human being who is constantly growing and changing, you have varied needs that are difficult to be met by only one person. It wasn't until I got into my thirties that I realized I had a misconception about giving and that my earlier expectations of my husband were unrealistic. You can't place such a huge burden on anyone to make you happy, not even a spouse.

Ironically, we are socialized to believe that somehow the person you fall in love with will meet all your needs perfectly, often without you even having to communicate what your needs are. What a lie! And the movies and novels have helped spread this narrative that many have bought into.

No one human being is able to fulfill all your needs; not your parents, spouse, children, best friend—no one. This is because we have such multiple needs: spiritual, financial, emotional, intellectual, social that it would be impossible to expect one person to meet all these needs. What a tall order!

According to a research done by an Australian nurse; Bronnie Ware, who spent years working in palliative care, one of the top five regrets of the dying is that they did not let themselves be happier. Many of them said they did not realise until the end of their life, that happiness is a choice.

Such truths made me decide long ago that regardless of the disappointments I get from the people I love, I will still choose to be happy and to give anyway. A good example is whenever I feel my husband is giving me the silent treatment. That's when I best express my love to him by giving him all my attention, serving him and listening to him.

I remember while working at a nursing home in Canada, I took note of an old man who despite accumulating enough assets in his life still seemed very lonely and sad. His children, he said, were too busy to give him the attention he desired. At one time he indicated that all he wanted was someone to spend time with and talk to, even if it's over lunch hour, just so that he could fill the void that he felt.

Moved by this, I tried to get my superiors at the nursing home to allow me to spend time with him after the usual day's routines but unfortunately it was against the organization's rules. However, I still interacted with the old man during the usual work sessions.

I was sad to learn that he later committed suicide in his bath tab. This old man taught me a lesson in life. I resolved to try and always give time to people especially when they are at their lowest in life. I've done my best to teach my children this virtue too. I also advocate for balance in life and that includes knowing your limits in giving so that you don't end up either emotionally, physically, spiritually or financially drained.

The best way to measure your giving at different levels of any relationship is to be honest with yourself about your motive for giving. Always give out of love. Try and give in such a manner that your giving transforms someone's life. If anything give to a person who you know can never repay you.

Fun and laughter during my bridal shower

Chapter 7

Priorities always keep changing.

If it's important to you, you will find a way.
If it's not you will find an excuse.
– Jim Rohn

IN MY FORTIES, I CAN totally appreciate indeed priorities do change, based on my personal experiences. This is because as you age, you get to different seasons of your life which demand for different things after all change is the only constant thing in life.

When you are young your focus will often be to work hard and acquire material assets. And this was the case with me. My mid-twenties were consumed with determination to get a new car and possibly even own a home. I also had a very ambitious plan to retire at the age of 30. I must admit I was able to get a car, an old one though, but I still never gave up on my dream of owning a new one.

One day, Martin and I were driving to the airport to pick up a friend who was visiting us. At the time, we lived in the US. All along I didn't have any suspicions that my husband was planning a surprise gift for me.

So, on our way back after picking my friend from the airport Martin suggested we take a detour which led us to a car yard. And that was when it finally dawned on me that I was getting a car, a new one as a matter of fact.

At last one my longest dreams had come true. In the days that followed, the feeling of excitement engulfed me. I couldn't get enough of the new car experience; from the smell of the car, its interior and the new tires. I remember driving it slowly afraid of having even a scratch let alone a dent on it. Everything about the new car excited me.

However, a few weeks later, the thrill of the new car had started to fade off. If anything it became a source of conflict between my daughter and I as I was always more worried about her spilling food in the car than actually enjoying the time we would spend together as we rode along.

This was the same case with my first time to travel to the UK. Despite it being a childhood dream, the thrill ended a few months after I arrived in the UK and quickly realized it wasn't a bed of roses as I thought.

This is a huge misconception among many young people who blindly think that being abroad is everything. It's not! But this just goes to show that many still believe the grass is greener on the other side. The reality is that the grass is greener where it is watered.

When martin and I first arrived in the US as a young couple having relocated from the UK, we had to sleep on the floor in an empty apartment for two months until we could afford some furniture. As much as Sandra, who at the time was too young to understand our predicament, enjoyed the idea of sleeping on the floor, we knew that we had to work quite hard to get whatever we needed and turn the space into a home.

Then there was a time when owning a big house was very important to me. It was all I wanted and I worked day and night to make sure that by the time I was 30 I would have a place to call mine that I designed from scratch. My greatest financial milestone was when I first built my house in Kenya without having to take up a loan. But trust me, I worked so hard for years abroad doing double shifts, sixteen hours, six days a week to save some money. For years, I had to forego a lot of things and survive on rice and beans in order to save as much as possible. There is nothing easy in life and you have to make sacrifices and work very hard to attain the things you want in life. Here's the thing now in my forties all I want is a small house that is full of love. Big is no longer important. See how priorities change? I'm a strong believer that one should do whatever makes them happy today, and plan for tomorrow, as long as you don't allow it to consume you and steal your day.

Now, having travelled in quite a number of countries, I can appreciate that home is where you heart is. The concept of greener pastures has nothing to do with where someone lives but rather the positive attitude they have about themselves and their circumstances as well as the choice to be happy regardless.

Most things, especially material things that we find ourselves straining to acquire so much in our mid twenties and thirties won't matter much in your forties, especially if they were not geared to build you as a person. It's never about things but about you as an individual.

Some parents work hard and deny themselves so much in life while chasing for wealth. In the process they deny their loved ones the gift of spending quality time together. Others overdo it by even financially supporting their grown up children, even though those children have what it takes to be financially independent.

In the same breathe; many parents are a guilty of breaking their backs to leave behind a financial inheritance for their children. Sadly in many of such instances long after the parent is departed, squabbles erupt between children fighting for the same inheritance their parents worked hard to leave behind. What a tragedy!

If only the departed had given their time to his children to enjoy and while at it imparted the value of hard work then they would have lived a more fulfilling life.

In an article, published on www.dailyworld.com on September 3, 2017, Pope Francis reminds parents not to kill themselves trying to leave an inheritance for their family. He says those benefits should be earned by each person, so parents need not dedicate their life to accumulating money, rather they should enjoy every waking minute that God has afforded you.

My beautiful home

Chapter 8

A mountain to one is a walk in the park for another.

Our greatest weakness lies in giving up. To succeed try just one more time.
– Thomas A. Edison

BEFORE JUDGING PEOPLE IT IS always advisable to try and see things from their point of view. This reminds me how several times I have noticed that there seems to be something really bothering my children. Yet each time I asked them about it, they would deny and simply say they are fine. That is until they are ready to open up about their worries with me. When they do, I find myself amused and many times I have dismissed some of their worries as insubstantial. Yet to them, at that particular time, whatever they were worried about was a really big deal to them.

Not too long ago my daughter Sandra got duped of a colossal amount of money in an online scam. In addition she maxed-out her phone credit card. Stressed and afraid of disappointing her parents she decided to keep this to herself and find a way out of the situation. Her best attempts were to take a gap year from university and try getting a job, which would then allow her to repay her credit without Martin and I finding out the truth. Something about her desire to take a gap year from university didn't add up because I knew she enjoyed it so much. We probed her further and assured her of our unwavering love and support. I remember how amidst tears, she opened up to us about the trouble she had got in. As I listened to her, I realized she was a child and prone to make mistakes and as her parents we chose to be graceful with her because no one is perfect. However I was convinced there was more to this story. It wasn't so much what she was telling us, but more about what she wasn't saying. A few days later as I sat with her over a diner date I learnt this was her cry for attention; she missed her mother and confidant so much. You see the last two years I have had to operate between Kenya; where I run my spa business and Canada, where my family lives. No doubt, this has been tough on my entire family but such is life and we are learning how to make the best of the situation one day at a time. Some days are tougher than others.

Over the years, I have learnt that one of the fastest ways to lose a relationship with your children, have them shut you out of their lives, give up and stop confiding in you about their difficulties is when they constantly do not feel like they are being heard. And this also applies to any other relationship one maybe in.

I have therefore become very intentional about creating opportunities for people to hear each other out in my house. We strive to create a safe space to talk to each other about whatever is bothering us, even when it's uncomfortable. No topic is a taboo in my house. I believe that if we can figure out a way to always talk to each other about what is bugging one, then we can always work on the issue and find a solution together. We are not perfect and many times we don't always get it right, but the most important thing is we keep at it.

It is natural for human beings to be too quick to judge even when we don't know one's full story. Often we expect people to be like us, think like us and even live by a certain script only approved by us; yet we are all different, and thereby will think and act differently and we shouldn't victimize those who seem to struggle in areas that we don't.

This lack of tolerance is especially visible in the differing political opinions between our political leaders. Currently in Kenya, we see it everyday, this being an election year. And it has even gone a notch higher after the nullification of the August 2017 presidential elections. The war of words between leaders, the lack of compromise with each party taking a hard stance, breakdown of dialogue, threats against each other, a lot of propaganda and mudslinging each other, it is just too toxic.

It is this same lack of tolerance that we see in Kenya when it comes to tribal matters. This takes me back to the 2007 post-election violence that erupted in Kenya. At the time, my family had returned to Kenya on holiday. I remember my children, who were both born abroad where tribe is a non-issue feeling confused about the stories in media of people attacking each other on basis of tribe.

For the first time in her life, Sandra, who was 10 years old asked me, "Mum what tribe are you? Are they going to kill us now if we belong to either of the tribes that are fighting each other in Kenya now? In disbelief and with tears welled up in my eyes, both Martin and I reassured her that we belonged to a tribe called Kenya and she needed not to worry because as citizens we have every right to be in the country.

However as news spread of people being killed, houses being torched and neighbours turning against each other, the more worried Sandra became. She demanded that we return home in the US because she didn't feel safe in Kenya anymore. This broke my heart because truth be told Kenya is my home and I love it. But I love my children even more and with the episodes that followed day after day, we left Kenya and relocated to Canada, a country that now my family and I call home.

I admit being tolerant of the other person takes a deliberate effort. In my early years of marriage my husband would sometimes come home distressed about work. When he would share with me what was stressing him, rather than just listen and allow him to vent, sometimes I would downplay the issue he was stressing about, without really being sensitive and hence end up in a conflict with him.

The truth is that we don't always see and resolve issues from the same perspective. Even when two people are faced with a similar issue, they are likely to have two different approaches towards the matter at hand. And when we are constantly having conflicts, it is easy to get frustrated, fed up and even give up on the relationship.

All relationships are a labour of love whether it is with your spouse, children, parents, siblings or friends. And if anything in the face of misunderstanding running away from the issue often feels the easier option.

But you have to keep trying one more time, until both parties get a common rhythm. If there is anyone in my life who is the epitome of never giving up but instead trying just one more time, then it has to be my younger brother Daniel. He has been my biggest inspiration in life.

Growing up Daniel was always a sickly baby. He was often skinny no matter how healthy my mother fed him. Despite the constant visits to hospitals, the doctors always gave him a clean bill of health. Although mum had a hunch that there was something off about Daniel's health, she couldn't point a finger at what exactly was wrong with him.

While in campus, Daniel was constantly on medication. He suffered severe skin break out, would contract boils from time to time, yet no doctor could tell what the source of these was. His medical situation non-withstanding he went on to make a huge success of himself in his academic education and got an admission to university. And even then he performed excellently and acquired a scholarship to further his studies at a Masters degree level.

His success has always served as an inspiration for me to make the most of my life. In a sudden turn of events, while on a routine annual health check-up, Daniel was diagnosed with a severe heart defect in early 2017. For the next few weeks Daniel and I towed from one hospital to another where he went through several tests in a bid to re-confirm the diagnosis.

All the tests confirmed that he had a heart defect. So dire was the condition that he was required to undergo an open heart surgery as soon as possible. Unbelievably, Daniel had this heart defect from birth only that it had never been detected and diagnosed before this and would manifest itself in various ways including suffering from skin conditions and being sickly constantly.

I accompanied my brother to India for the surgery and prayed he would survive it. Even as they wheeled him away into the theatre, I prayed that the surgery would be successful. I remember watching him after the eight-hour long surgery that felt like a lifetime. He lay motionless on his bed in the Intensive care unit (ICU). The strong man I knew and always looked up to looked nothing close to the man I saw fighting for his life desperately. Daniel was frail and now looked up to me to be strong and pray for his recovery.

Tears raced down my cheeks. I would pray for him and speak to him reminding him that he had been down so many times before and each time he arose stronger. Even then I needed him to fight for his life and come out stronger than before. I was desperate.

Daniel did not wake up immediately after his surgery. In that moment, one of my biggest fears was that if he did not pull through, my parents would never forgive me for keeping them in the dark. Because the events leading to his surgery had taken place quite fast and we had no time to let my parents know about his condition in a face to face conversation, my siblings and I agreed that we would keep this information to ourselves. The plan was to inform my parents soon after the successful surgery.

Even though Daniel was unconscious, I still camped by his bedside and would talk to him. I urged him to fight for his life because his family still needed him. I was too weak to pray so I just kept chanting God's name. However, I knew my family were praying and fasting because I felt strong even though I was weak. Truly just like the bible says, God is our strength when we are weak.

Looking back, I have no idea how I was able to stay up for a week; from the day of Daniel' surgery, to the day he was admitted at the Intensive Care Unit where he was unconscious, to finally regaining his consciousness and being able to sit up on his bed.

Today, Daniel, who is 40 years old, is referred to as the miracle baby. Unbelievably he has suffered a heart defect since birth that went undiagnosed for 40 years.

How he survived remains a miracle that even baffles him. I am so thankful that the heart surgery was successful and in a week's time he could sit up on his bed. God gave him a second chance at life. Daniel is truly nothing short of a miracle! He has become my testimony that when all else fails tap into your inner strength.

Later, I had a conversation with Daniel about the time when death seemed to stare at him. From the conversation, it was obvious that many times when you are healthy you don't think much about the gift of life until when faced with mortality.

"At that moment, not even your money is of much use to you as it can't buy you life. You think about your loved ones whom you may never get a chance to spend time with again and wonder if they know how much you love them. You worry about how they will cope with your demise," Daniel says.

He goes on to explain that, "Your heart breaks for your children, you wonder how they will grow up and pray that they will not suffer when you are no longer there to shield them from pain. You ask yourself whether you touched lives and made an impact and wonder how and if at all you will be remembered. You think about all the unfulfilled dreams you kept postponing. It is such a scary feeling."

Daniel's heart condition made me realise how fragile life is. We promised each other that we would use our experience in India to create awareness on the important of parents insisting that their children have an echocardiography (echo) test at birth.

An echo is an ultrasound scan of the heart using special machines that give an accurate view of the heart. The scan helps to detect any heart abnormalities, enabling doctors to work on rectifying the situation. Usually, the scan takes an average of 20 minutes and is painless. One need not have any special preparation for the scan, as it is not a surgical procedure. In fact, you can eat and drink normally before and even after the scan. The scan is important because it can help avoid a situation like that of Daniel, whereby you suffer a heart defect for years that goes unnoticed.

Sad thing is that while in India we met a young couple from Kenya who had brought their seven month old baby for a heart surgery to rectify an abnormality. For the two weeks we were at the hospital, we interacted with them and a bond was formed. However in a tragic turn of events, when the baby underwent the surgery, things took a turn for the worse. Daniel and I received news of the demise of this baby, a few months after our interaction. Our hearts broke.

I couldn't understand why God would take home such a young, innocent life. I started feeling guilty that my brother survived the surgery while the baby didn't. Daniel too was heartbroken because he had formed a special bond with this family, having shared a similar tribulation. All the same he kept reminding me that God still remains God even when we couldn't understand his ways.

I had so many questions, one of which is why bad things happen to good people. Losing a loved one is a devastating thing and the pain is beyond words. But I turned to the word of God for answers.

The bible reminds me that just because one is a Christian does not automatically mean they will have an easy life. But what one is guaranteed is an eternal life and those who depart in faith go to a better place. John 14:1-4 "Do not let your hearts be troubled. You believe in God; believe also in me. My Father's house has many rooms; if that were not so, would I have told you that I am going there to prepare a place for you? And if I go and prepare a place for you, I will come back and take you to be with me that you also may be where I am. You know the way to the place where I am going."

Chapter 9

Money does not buy you happiness.

To pretend to satisfy one's desires by possessions
is like using straw to put off a fire.
– Chinese proverb

JUST BECAUSE ONE IS WEALTHY, doesn't mean one is happy. Money is good, it gets you by and you can enjoy some pleasures of life with it. However, it cannot buy happiness, peace of mind or true love and friendship.

This reminds me of my days as a nurse in Canada at a nursing home. There were quite a number of rich, old people who we were being taken care of at the nursing home; giving them the best service that their money could afford them. However, many of these had such a sad and lonely life even after accumulating so much wealth in life.

I have also seen how money can destroy relationships and steal peace in the family. For instance the same money that you lend a friend, a family member or a business associate is the same that has the power to complicate those relationships if there is betrayal such as unkept promises to refund it.

In that regard I have learnt to live by certain rules when it comes to money and relationships. One such rule is not to lend that which I am unwilling to lose in the event that it's not refunded.

In 2004 my brother and I decided to start a printing business in Kenya. At the time I was living in the US while he lived in the UK. We both agreed to relocate to Kenya. My husband would join us as soon as the business picked up.

However, when I reported to work on the first day, I felt lost and unfulfilled. I knew nothing about the printing business and it was not the area of my strength. I was just following the business trend at the time and advice from people that the printing business was next big thing in Kenya. What a huge mistake!

When I couldn't take it anymore, I gave my blessing to my brother to run the business and flew back to the US. Eventually, he also realized this was not his passion and with that he closed shop.

Back in the US, from time to time I would have a heart- to-heart with my husband about how unhappy and unfulfilled I was with life. By 2007, my marriage was getting strained as my husband couldn't understand what I really wanted. To be honest even I was not sure about what I wanted.

Life was good since we had acquired most of the things we wanted to but I still felt a deep void. Eventually I convinced my husband we should consider relocating to Kenya, this time we would go together.

Despite all the sacrifices we had made to save up and acquire some assets, Martin, in his usual loving and supportive nature agreed to this plan. We began the preparation for our relocation and within a year, we sold most of our assets and came back to Kenya. I had fulfilled my desire and expected to settle back home, happy.

Unbelievable as this may seem our stay in Kenya was short lived. Barely six months into the country, both of us didn't want to stay anymore. We were unhappy. We were back to the drawing board, this time we set out again to figure ourselves out in a different country. Having money is not everything, it cannot buy you happiness.

Many people dream of winning the lottery and imagine if that were to happen their lives would change for the better. They would be at their happiest because they could afford all the niceties in the world. In many ways this view is shaped by the media, but the reality depicts a totally different picture.

Stories have been told of people who have won sporting bets, lotteries or gained huge inheritance that changed their financial status. Sadly, most of these stories have an unhappy ending.

The American Psychology Association (APA) posted a study done by Robert Kenny, a developmental psychologist and senior advisor.

The research was on aspirations, dilemmas and personal philosophies of the wealthy multimillionaires. The survey indicated that while money eased many aspects of their lives, it also made other aspects more difficult.

The researchers found that the greatest aspirations of the responders was to be good parents. They said money helped them get the best schools for their children, but were concerned how their children were perceived by other children as rich kids. Money and their children's perspective of money was a concern.

The conclusion of the research was that the responders' major concern was not money but the social welfare of their children and being good parents to them. Having a lot of money is great, don't get me wrong, but just know it comes with some downsides and you can't buy happiness with it.

My first job as a nurse at the Royal Hospital, London

Chapter 10

Parenting is a full time job

Children can be a source of greatness or an excuse
to give up on your dreams.
– Unknown

CHILDREN ARE A BLESSING AND often bring a great sense of joy. When I had my first child; Sandra while I was still in my early twenties she became my priority and the driving force in everything that I attempted. I wanted to give her the best life that I could possibly offer her and exactly four months after I had her, I decided to go back to work.

I had a deep conviction that it would be more fulfilling for both me and my daughter if I was working and raising her at the same time. My job at the time was a night-shift job and we agreed with my husband that I would stay and take care of her during the day while he went to work and we could role-play this in the evening. Taking care of our child by ourselves was great since it allowed us to spend more time with her and understand her better.

In any case hiring the services of a nanny in the UK was unaffordable for us at the time.

Many times work and motherhood have been construed as being in opposition. Some people actually believe you can't do both, that one will suffer at the expense of another.

My experience has been that both are attainable with a strong supportive system around you. Often society judges women a bit too harsh as some of the expectations placed on them are unfair because different women are faced with different motherhood situations. For instance many people assume that a stay-at-home mother does no work at home which is not true.

There is a lot of pressure for one to be a super mum who can do it all. And so, many mothers end up feeling as failures for not being able to balance career, motherhood, marriage, among other roles that demand of their time. It takes a lot of courage to stand strong and refuse to be defined by the expectations of others. Many women deep down just want the choice to decide what is right for them without being dictated to by everyone else what they should do or who they should be.

There is nothing wrong with being a stay-at-home mum. However, if getting a child is the reason or excuse for you to give up on your dream, then that's the greatest injustice you could do to yourself. I am a strong believer that both parents should be supportive in raising their children together without victimizing the other for wanting to pursue an aspiration at the same time.

Children should never be the excuse for one not to live their life fully and actualize their dreams. Research has shows that mothers who forgo their dreams are more likely to live their dreams through their children. Many of them end up meddling so much into their children's lives and as a result end up raising children who are so dependent on their parents and lack life skills to cope on their own.

One of the fundamental skills any parent should strive to build in their child is self esteem. In this era where achievement is held in high regard, sometimes unnecessarily, it is important to build your child's esteem. Some of the ways you can do this is by complimenting your child's efforts and being patient with progress rather than focusing on the end goal which is the achievement itself.

It is okay to allow your child to fail and even feel disappointed now and again, as this is a real way of preparing them for the real life when they're out of your nest. After all they need to know they will not always get their way.

Self esteem is important because when children are confident, it sets them up for success — in everything- such as academics, sports and friendships. They are keen to try new challenges and take pride in their abilities.

When my daughter Maxine was 8 years old, she was afraid of anything she felt was a challenge.

As a result she shielded herself from trying out new things such as playing a new sport, learning a new instrument or even making new friends. When I noticed this, I began reassuring her that it was always better to try and fail than not to try at all. With time her confidence levels built up and today, she is a confident pre-teen, who easily makes friends and is always willing to try out new stuff.

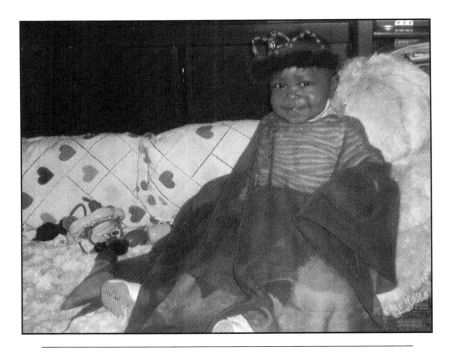

Maxine

Chapter 11

Build good relationship in all levels of life.

Even marriages made in heaven need down to earth maintenance work.
– Lloyd Byers

WHEN MARTIN AND I STARTED dating, we were so much in love that we couldn't see how anything could go wrong between us. I must admit though it has taken me 20 years to fully appreciate our wedding vows and to really understand what until death do us part means. Like fine wine, our love has matured with age.

My early memory of our marriage was having constant silly arguments. At the time, I remember getting upset with Martin, for his seemingly don't care attitude which I had identified while we were dating. Somehow I thought, like any other woman in her early twenties, I could change my husband, forgetting that the only person I had the power to change was me.

Thankfully by God's grace we were able to outlive those turbulent first years in marriage, considering that most couples get to breaking point during the initial five years. Now in his forties, Martin is quite a mellow man and my children view him as a very gentle and caring dad. But this wasn't always the case.

Any relationship requires lots of patience so as to explore all the options, grow and become better. This is true of a relationship between spouses, siblings and even friends. You will need to cultivate time together, be patient and understanding with each other, forgive each other severally, and be willing to give it a try one more time. And the same goes for family too.

Although many people enjoy a close relationship with family members, others don't for various reasons. Mine too hasn't always been a close-knit relationship.

At some point in my life, I felt as if I was born in the wrong family. This was after living abroad for years only to return home and feel like a stranger because I couldn't connect with some of my family members. Being blood relatives, I assumed that automatically we ought to connect and when we didn't it was frustrating. Thoughts of cutting links with my family crossed my mind.

However, when I got into my thirties, I remember having a strong desire to reconnect with my estranged family members. And so I made a deliberate move to reach out to them, and was patient with myself and them as we re-established a relationship.

Now I look back and I can't overstate just how important my family is to me. Family is priceless and it's a bond that should never be broken.

I truly believe that good relationships are the only cushion one can have at their weakest moment in life. My word of advice to anyone who cares to listen is that if you are estranged from your family or friend, put your pride aside, and reach out. And when you do, be kind to yourself and them as you mend your relationship back. Take one day at a time, without being judgmental or forceful. With time your relationship will fall in place. After all anything worthwhile in life takes time and effort.

Family vacation at Niagara falls

Enjoying our honeymoon

Chapter 12

Speak that which you want to come true.

Faith is like love: It is revealed only in action and word!
– Kenneth E. Hagin

THE TONGUE IS A VERY small organ yet it carries a lot of power. Even the Bible strongly emphasizes on this. Proverbs 18:2 Death and life are in the power of the tongue, and those who love it will eat its fruit. We therefore ought to watch out what comes from our mouth. Admittedly, this is not easy and takes a lot of self discipline. The tongue is capable of fuelling war and mediating peace.

Dreams are good and sometimes God uses them to communicate to us and even stir our imagination. However, until we speak about those dreams and be bold to take action on them, they remain only that- dreams.

Job 22; 28 Thou shall decree a thing, and it shall be established and the light shall shine upon thy ways. This means that as long as you state to the lord what your heart desires and meditate on what His will for you is, then your desires will come to pass.

Many Christians are unaware of how much power and authority has been given to them by the mere fact that they are children of God. We have the power and the authority to speak out a thing in our life and expect to see it manifested.

That is what faith is about, but many of us do not exercise this. To decree and declare a thing and expect to see the manifestation, one must know the word of God and the only way to do so is to read your bible.

A perfect example of how words have power is the Apple brand and its iPhone product. The brand stands out thanks to their marketing prowess that captures the imagination of their clients by describing features of the device before it is even in the market. As a result, people anticipate for it, line up and camp outside the Apple stores for hours whenever a new version of Iphone is about to released to the market, based on what they have heard about the phone.

Words have power and hence why we should be careful to always speak blessings into our lives and that of others. The desire of God is for us to use our tongues to bring glory to his name and to advance his kingdom.

When my family and I first came to Canada, we knew God but didn't have a close relationship with Him. After we settled down, we looked for a local church where we could plug in. This led us to Faith Alive Christian Centre under the pastoral leadership of Pastor Lennox John Smithin, who took my family in and nurtured us into the mature Christians we are today.

Time and again Pastor Lennox would preach about speaking life into the things that one desires to come to pass. I took this message to heart. And when I ventured into the Amway business in Canada, the same principal was advocated. Being the audacious person that I am, I decided to test it. Looking back I can testify that there truly is power in the tongue. The life I live today and my achievements are what I saw with my eyes of faith and spoke of, as if they already were in existence eight years ago. The Lord has fulfilled most of my heart's desires.

In addition to speaking life into the things we desire we also need to act. Many people pray about certain situations in their life but fail to take action. God responds to faith and action. James 2:14-17 Dear friends, do you think you'll get anywhere in this if you learn all the right words but never do anything? Does merely talking about faith indicate that a person really has it? For instance, you come upon an old friend dressed in rags and half-starved and say, "Good morning, friend! Be clothed in Christ! Be filled with the Holy Spirit!" and walk off without providing so much as a coat or a cup of soup—where does that get you? Isn't it obvious that God-talk without God-acts is outrageous nonsense?

Even as you pray there is need to act. I believe the first step of action in life is to show up. This shows at least you are making the effort and from there you are able to keep making the steps needed towards achieving any goal you put your mind into.

During my time in the Amway business, I recall introducing a young woman into the business. At first she was very apprehensive to join the business stating that she had no car to move around and attend Amway business meetings. In addition, she did not know how to drive and was scared at the thought of driving herself. Since I believed in the business model and had even tested it out, I encouraged her to join with the assurance that if she worked hard she would save enough to even buy a car. For the next few weeks I volunteered to give her a lift to the meetings on condition that she would enroll into a driving school. She did. I held her hand in the business showing her the ropes and true by the end of that year not only had she learnt to drive but she had also saved enough money to enable her purchase a second-hand car. Truly no dream in life is too big for God. Prayer and taking action towards your dreams will eventually see you succeed.

Chapter 13

Get rid of toxic people in your life.

Life is too short to waste your time on people who don't respect, appreciate and value you
– Roy T. Bennet

GETTING TOXIC PEOPLE OUT OF one's life might prove challenging especially if they are people close to you such as family members. But all the same you're as good as the people you hang out with. Studies have shown that you are the average of the five people you spend most of your time with.

In my younger years having just gotten to the UK, the friends I made played a huge role in influencing my lifestyle both positively and negatively. With some, I would hang out with them and for the first time in my life, I started taking alcohol, while others took me to church and encouraged me to further my studies and make something out of my life.

After re-evaluating my life I started prioritizing certain things. Drinking alcohol and clubbing every other weekend was not appealing to me anymore.

I took a hard stance that I would not fall into peer pressure but instead would influence my friends positively, with every chance I got. This included Martin, who was my boyfriend then and quite the life of the party. My first strategy was to make a list of all my family members and friends and then audit if their influence on me was positive or negative. Those who were toxic but I couldn't get rid of, I purposed to spend the least amount of time with them.

Toxic people are energy suckers and will leave you feeling tired and miserable. Many times they are overly critical, always complain, and find fault with everyone and everything in their lives. Their view of life, people and situations is from a negative perspective and are always demanding something from you without ever adding value. Nothing is ever good enough for them.

It is important to avoid such people at all cost and if that is not possible reduce the amount of time you spend with them. Alternatively, if you choose to spend time with them have a strategy of how you can influence them positively. Otherwise you may end up being negatively influenced or drained.

In life you have to be the change you want to see. It is very easy to sit back and watch as things go wrong and talk about the perpetrators behind their back. However, you first have to acknowledge that you have the power to change and influence situations. For instance if you are in a conversation whose tone and theme is negative, you can choose to join in the negative talk or change the conversation into a positive one.

Our goal in life should be to add value to other people's lives every time we have a chance to. When you see someone doing something wrong, it is always better to approach them in a kind way and correct them. You may be surprised that they are not aware their actions offend others.

Chapter 14

When going after your dreams, sacrifice will be required.

Luck is a dividend of sweat. The more you sweat the luckier you get.
– Ray Kroc

NO PAIN, NO GAIN. THIS is a truth I have learnt throughout my life whenever it was time to move from one stage to the next. I first experienced it when I moved from Kenya to the UK as a teenager. And then I experienced it yet again in 2015, when I left Canada to return to Kenya and start my medical spa business. My husband and children remained behind, which is the biggest sacrifice I have had to make in life.

To be honest, if I chose to focus on pain and sacrifice, then perhaps I would still be stuck in the village in Nanyuki. Tough as it may be, a beautiful life has emerged out of it. Today, I am living my dream, my family is happy and we strive to live a balanced life daily. Being away has made my children learn to be independent and I hope they have seen the value of hard work firsthand.

If there is an important value, I hope to I have demonstrated and pass on to my children it is that hardwork wins over talent, when talent fails to work hard. It doesn't matter how gifted you are at something, or what brilliant ideas you have. If you never put the talents and the ideas to action and work on them consistently, you are as good as dead.

And this value is especially key to the millennials as this is the generation that has grown up with gadgets which have simplified tasks for them. As a result, they are very impatient with many believing one can acquire anything in life instantly. They know little or nothing about delayed gratification.

I often admire sportsmen and believe we all can learn from them. By the time we get to see them win awards in international arenas, chant their names with pride, and even want to associate with their success, many of us are unaware of the sacrifices that they have made behind the scenes. For instance athletes undergo rigorous training routines. They have to endure the cold morning, a few hours of sleep and long hours of practice often in harsh terrains. In addition they have to maintain a certain level of fitness as a well as stick to a strict, healthy diet. By the time they win medals, a lot of hardwork has been put in.

And when they lift their trophies to celebrate nothing else matters. The gains among sportsmen just like in life come from pushing yourself, making sacrifices, believing in you and never giving up. It doesn't matter how tough the challenge you face may seem and how many times you fall, as long as you rise up, dust yourself and keep trying one more time, you will eventually win in life.

I hope my children will take this important lesson into their adult life and reach for their stars. I am reminded of my experience in 2015 when I returned to Kenya ready to launch Timeless Medical Spa. I has shipped the needed products and equipment and found space to let at a Mall in Nairobi's uptown market. However I needed to fix up the interior of the rental space.

Through a referral, I ended up hiring an architect to take charge of the design and construction of the spa. However, six months into it, I was met by the sight of a poorly done interior and an architect who has swindled me of my money and disappeared. Never mind the project had cost me time as well as a massive amount of money. I couldn't believe it.

I remember sitting at the rental space, frustrated at the lack of answers. I broke down and cried hysterically, confused about what to do next. At that point, throwing in the towel felt much easier.

I was afraid of trying again only to fail miserably. The fear of the unknown was holding me back. However with time I realised if I gave up on the idea of the spa, I would be more frustrated than if I tried again and failed.

Weeks later, with the encouragement of my mother, I recollected myself, sought the services of a different architecture to fix up the spa. In July 2015, I opened the doors of Timeless Medical Spa in Nairobi's Lavington mall. Today, I look back at the business and the success that has come from it, and I am glad that I pushed on despite the initial hitches. I dread to think what would have become of me and this business if I had given up.

At times, we are scared to pursue our dreams because we think there should be a common script for all. But that is not true. We all are unique individuals who think differently, have different paths and vision. Therefore there is no one- fit -all script when it comes to life. Sometimes you actually need to break the rules for you to truly know your full potential. As long as you are authentic you will stand out, grow and discover things that you wouldn't if you stuck to the norm.

My decision to return to Kenya, leave behind my family and set up a business is so untraditional.

In many African homes the norm is that men go to look for greener pastures and leave behind their wives and children. In my case, it is different. Many people did not understand this and termed it unacceptable just because it was unconventional. Rumors of all sorts went around in a bid to try and make sense of the situation. But I had the blessing of both my husband and my children and that was all that mattered. They understood how much actualizing my dream meant to me. If I had paid attention to what people thought was the right thing for me to do, my dream would still be in the pipeline and many Kenyans would be missing out on my services.

For anyone who is trying to break the rules and finding it difficult, my advice is listen to your inner voice because at the end of the day it is your life and trying to please others will leave you miserable.

I guess I have never been one who is afraid to go against the grain. I believe it is important to be true to yourself. For instance 24 years ago, against the wishes of most of my family members, I married Martin Mbuthia. According to some of them, Martin did not fit into their idea of what would be a perfect husband for me. Today, we have two beautiful daughters and a full life and I could not have chosen a better partner. If I could do it again

I would marry the same man. If breaking the rules means following your heart, then by all means go for it. Today, my husband has a very good relationship with my family, as they eventually warmed up to him.

Chapter 15

Life is a dance, find your space.

When you dance to your own rhythm, life taps its toes to your own beat
– Terri Guillemets

DIFFERENT GENRES OF MUSIC HAVE different rhythms to dance to and the same goes for life. One has to figure out their rhythm and dance to it and when it changes we shouldn't be hesitant to adjust or learn a new one.

Sometimes just when you think you have figured out stuff in your life or have things in place, life throws a curve ball at you. You should always be ready and willing to adjust in order to suit the different situations in life. On the same breathe there is no point to focus on one's weaknesses either. There is no right or wrong way of living life and there are no regrets in life, only lessons.

I remember my first experience learning to swim was so horrible that at some point I felt like it wasn't for me. Eventually, I gathered courage and kept trying till I figured it out. I had dreaded the experience because of my earlier failed attempts. But like the saying goes one can never know your full potential without taking risks.

Many times we like to operate on the periphery and when we attempt to figure something once and miss it, we tend to dismiss it all together. We are so afraid of going deeper and this is true even of our interactions with others. It is no wonder these days a lot of relationships do not hold for long. What you see when you meet people for the first time is often only 20 per cent of who they truly are, because the 80 per cent is barely discovered. Hence why, it is necessary to connect with people at a deeper level for you to know who they truly are. And this takes time and patience but it's the only way to truly know people.

I remember sometime back when I began to feel a void and could tell that something was missing in my life. However I down played it and acted as if everything was okay. Even when my husband suspected it, still he thought it was mostly because of work-related stress. I lost weight and my skin started to break out but still I pretended that everything was okay.

At some point in our marriage, Martin and I disconnected for a couple of months and it felt like we were two strangers living together. This was until I initiated an engagement that required the two of us sit down and open up to each other about what was really bugging us. This led us to seek counseling and enabled us to re-connect. That experience taught me not to wait until things are broken so as to seek help.

My inspiration to write this book has been to change lives positively through my life experiences. In my forties, I feel I'm at the peak of my life and hence my resolve to share my life with others through this book, and connect with people at a greater depth and hopefully transform at least one person's life.

Chapter 16

Giving your children everything doesn't mean you love them.

An infallible way to make your child miserable is to satisfy all his demands.
– Henry Home

FROM MY PERSONAL EXPERIENCE WITH my kids I've learnt that by giving everything to your children, you actually cripple them because you deny them both their independence and the freedom to discover themselves. This leaves them entirely dependent on you. They grow up into little brats, who feel entitled and walk around acting like the world owes them something, when the truth is nobody owes them anything!

In this day and age, it is ironic that gadgets are a big thing yet at the same time they are the greatest distraction for kids. Many parents feel guilty about their busy lifestyles today that sometimes keeps them them away from home thereby eating into the time they would have been spending with their children. As a result, they go into a retail therapy spree to compensate for the guilt they feel.

But they shouldn't kill themselves just to impress their kids or even allow their children to manipulate them into getting anything they want. Once in a while, kids should be allowed to work for what they want as it gives them an early opportunity to appreciate hard work.

I have seen some marriages break because parents can't seem to agree on how best to raise their kids. From the decision of what school to take their kids to, when to buy them a car, what food they should eat, which household chores, if any, they should do. It gets even harder when one parent's idea of parenting does not agree with that of the other. This is especially in situations where one parent is trying to impress their child by giving them everything they ask for regardless of the need.

Some parents actually think the more things they give their children the more their children will love them back. What a myth!

While in the US, I once worked with a lady who did sixteen hours shift, seven days a week. She never took a day off, not even once, so that she could give her kids the latest material things; a phone, latest shoes and clothes. She was always miserable because of sleep deprivation. When I asked her what would happen to her if she became unwell and could no longer work or worse if she fell down and died and thus couldn't offer her children even her presence, she stared at me and said she hoped that would never happen. Whereas it is great to give gifts to children, these should always be done within reason.

Rather than gifting children every time, there is need to teach them how to survive in the world. Let them know there is competition in the world. Whether in business or any other set up in life, healthy competition is important. It helps to improve the quality of services in business and keeps minds engaged. It is also an opportunity to create relationships and gives one the drive for excellence.

Without a little competition you do not grow and get fulfillment in life, instead you become stagnant because you always think you're the best and only you deserve a win in life.

Used wisely, competition can accelerate growth and make you think outside the box. For example when I was in the multi-level marketing business in Amway, we were always competing for achiever pins which signified that we were gaining momentum in the business and climbing the hierarchy and making more money. If there wasn't any competition among ourselves the motivation and growth would be lost.

With this I learned a very important lesson that to move to the next level in life, a little competition is inevitable. Also this separates the weak from the strong; it is another way of you gauging your strength.

In sports, if one team loses they go home and work hard to improve themselves in order to become winners at the next game. If there was no competition then sports would be boring. And life is the same way too.

Chapter 17

Loving and taking care of yourself.

The real opportunity for success lies with the person and not the job.
– Zig Ziglar

WHEN I WAS YOUNGER, I overlooked the number of hours I slept and to some point my eating habits were bad. I remember at one time I fell so ill while I was driving. I was literally throwing up as I drove. On being admitted in hospital, the doctors could tell that I was under a lot of stress and pressure. Since then I've learnt to create some alone time every week where I shut myself out from the hectic routines and I distress either by reading a book or catching up with an old friend. Creating time for oneself to rediscover and rejuvenate is vital for everyone.

It is also important to adopt an active lifestyle and a healthy diet. When you are young, the idea of eating a healthy diet and keeping fit is unpopular and doesn't feel very important. But as you get older, you begin to fully appreciate the benefits of an active lifestyle and a healthy diet.

The misconceptions that working out means going to the gym is misleading. People should be creative and work with whatever is within their environment and means. This may involve simple things such as avoiding to use the lifts when at work and instead taking the stairs, getting away from your desk to stretch and even go for a walk, drinking more water instead of fizzy drinks, including fruits and vegetables as part of your diet and reducing your food portions.

Taking care of yourself also includes surrounding yourself with those that love and uplift you and establishing healthy ways to bond. Being abroad away from many of our family meant that we had to learn to enjoy our company as we hadn't made many friends abroad. Our weekends were spent hanging out and spending quality time together. We also cultivated the habit of praying together as a family. This has helped to create a good spiritual foundation for my children.

No matter how busy life gets, setting time to pray and eat together as a family creates such a deep bond amongst members of a family. It also fosters openness through conversations in the family.

With today's world where it's all about gadgets, I've realized that if one is not cautious you can be in the same room as a family and no one is in sync with the other. One person could be on their phone, another on their or laptop and another on their Ipod or watching TV; all these within one room.

That's why I think it's very important to insist on setting time as a family to do bond over an activity and give each other the attention we all yearn for. Otherwise we risk raising families that do not know each other even though they live together.

I remember when growing up it was very important for my grandparents that once a year the whole family would be together to reconnect and get to know each other. Many times this happened over Christmas holiday or New Year. However, with some families choosing not to celebrate such traditions these days, you realise that cousins don't even know each other and uncles don't even know their nieces and nephews. How I wish people would stop replacing the face to face meetings with chats and texts at least once a while.

Memories of my young family

Chapter 18

Respect other people's choices.

Arguments always begin with an answer in mind.
Conversations begin with a question
– Unknown

WE SHOULDN'T MEASURE OTHER PEOPLE'S choices using our own expectations. Many times we place this burden on those close to us. When I married Martin, my dad felt that my husband couldn't match up to the standards he expected of the man that was going to marry me. This is because he had invested so much in me and felt that I deserved better. Not once did dad ask me how I felt about Martin; did I love him? Was he good to me? It took years for him to appreciate my choice and to also learn to accept my husband.

People should learn to respect other people's choices even if they are totally different from their preferences. In life most of the time we judge other people based on our own life and the lens we view life from, forgetting that what might look like a perfect life to us isn't the same for another person. It took me a long time to understand this because born and raised in Africa for eighteen years, the family values that I grew up with were totally different from those of the western world.

When I moved to the UK my sense of fashion, my approach to dating and lifestyle was totally different from what I saw there. I remember I found it strange how people openly showed their emotions in public. Kissing and holding hands in public was a taboo where I came from. I used to mistake that for lack of morals but little did I know that we are all socialized differently and every family has its own set of values and we should respect each other's choices.

Now that I have two children that are born abroad I have learned to respect some of the choices they make that I personally would not make because of the way I was raised and where I was raised. With them some things come easy while to me it's almost impossible. I used to force them to eat the kind of food I loved because I assumed they would love it too since it's the food my mother loved and raised me with. I came to realize that as long as they ate healthy the food they ate didn't have to be entirely my choice.

Sandra at school in Worcester MA

Chapter 19

It is okay to make mistakes sometimes.

Adversity does not build character, it reveals it.
– Heywood Brown

MOST GOOD THINGS THAT I now know of are those that I have learnt by making mistakes. I am not afraid to admit that I have made many. I've also discovered new recipes after I thought I used the wrong ingredient only to find out that my error was actually a better alternative.

Learning through mistakes makes you a better person. I know it sounds cliché but it is only a mistake if you did not learn from it, and if you repeat it. Before I learned what my purpose in life was I thought I could be a jack of all trades. I was that person who tried a hand at all sorts of businesses. Many of those businesses failed, because I was either trying to be somebody else or doing the business that was popular at the time. I kept swaying from one business to another and only learnt later that I needed to be consistent in one thing which I loved, pursue it fully and whole-heartedly if I was going to find any success.

One of the ways I knew something was off, were the comments I got from those I interacted with including my clients. They constantly told me my destiny was elsewhere because whenever something little went wrong the fire in me would burn out. However looking back, I realise all these mistakes shaped my character because now I can say I truly do what I love with all my heart and there is never a dull moment.

If it wasn't for the mistakes I made while trying out different things I would have never found my true calling and gift. Many of us strive for perfection in life. If anything, we dread mistakes and when we make them we get so embarrassed about it, we could literally die of it. But it is important to cut yourself some slack and acknowledge that as long as you are human mistakes are bound to be part of life. Accepting this is the first lesson in growing up because it opens you up to explore.

Knowing that if you mess up here and there it won't be the end of the world is the most liberating feeling. It frees you off fear. The fear of being nothing, achieving nothing and thereby becoming nothing should be way bigger than the fear of making mistakes.

Brittany Renée couldn't have said it better in this quote, "I would much rather have regrets about not doing what people said than regretting not doing what my heart led me to, and wondering what life would have been like, if I had just been myself.

Life is all about perceptions because while I choose to embrace my mistakes for leading me to my purpose someone else may choose to view it differently. Depending on your perception life can be as beautiful as you would like it to be or as unbearable as you choose to see it. You get to choose.

My husband was fully supportive of my decision to come to Kenya and start a business that was my passion, despite my past failures. If he was skeptical and insecure, he would not only have made me miss out on implementing my dream but also denied me of the opportunities that my business has opened not only for me but for our family, my staff and the many people from all walks of life whom we continue to serve.

I am a believer that we attract in life what we want. I have a friend who suffered from skin cancer and whenever I went to visits him he always looked happy. When I asked him why he was always happy despite his situation, he responded by saying that he had two choices; to be sad and gloomy or happy and optimistic and he chose the later.

Your past and current circumstances don't define your future. It doesn't matter what mistakes you have made in life or what limitations you have. Never allow these to deter you from achieving whatever you want in life. In my case I am very cognizant that I have a heavy mother-tongue accent. However I never allow this to stop me from being successful.

Building my business; Timeless Medical Spa has not been an easy journey. I get amused when I hear people who are not entrepreneurs themselves, talk about successful entrepreneurs in a fairly–tale, instant wealth and overnight success kind of way. This is not the reality. A lot of times businesses are built in struggle, sweat and tears, amidst lots of disappointments, and doubts as well as feelings of despair. My journey hasn't been any different.

When I first began the business I remember being very excited. I had worked as a nurse for years abroad doing double shifts, working 16 hours, six days a week to save some money that I could start my business with. I also had the blessing of my husband's input which was very helpful. In those years working as a nurse, I lived on rice and beans in order to save enough and see my dreams come true. This was a true test for me. There were moments when I wondered if my sacrifice was going to amount to anything worth writing home about. There were days I would be so frustrated and cry my heart out to God. It really helped that I am a person of faith because I don't know how I would otherwise push on.

There aren't many people who are willing to sacrifice and live below their financial means for a period of time in order to save some money for a better tomorrow, especially in a world of instant gratification. Whether you are just watching some television or walking into a mall or even just surfing the internet you will always be bombarded by advertisements of things you need to purchase now. Some of these are not even necessities but somehow you end up being swayed to spend and spend more money hence save less. I am glad I survived this.

When I had Ksh 25 million worth of savings, I began by writing down my dream and drawing up a business plan with a pen and paper. I truly believe in the power of writing down your goals. A study carried out by Dr. Gail Matthews, a psychology professor at the Dominican University in California, on the art and science of goal setting found out that you become 42 per cent more likely to achieve your goals and dreams, simply by writing them down on a regular basis. In addition, your chances of transforming your goals into a reality go further up once you share your written goals with a friend but not any kind of friend, a friend who believes in your ability to succeed. To me this is the power of the tongue because even the word of God says that life and death are in the power of the tongue. In my case I shared my dreams with my husband because he has always believed in me and cheered me on towards my dreams. He remains my biggest supporter.

I then carried out a market research on the various products in the market before settling on the one that would be my business product. I also had a look into the various manufacturing companies, in search of equipment for the spa. Like many entrepreneurs, this was an exciting time for me as I could visualize the business coming to life.

I knew it was in business that I could build wealth. Don't get me wrong, employment is important for one to learn and even build networks, and I was in employment for years before moving to business; however one can only build wealth in business. Whereas in employment your pay cheque is guaranteed, in business every month could be different, you write your own cheque. Having said that, I believe entrepreneurship is not for people who are unwilling to take calculated risks. From my experience, I have learnt that business pays more once it's established although it's tough in the beginning. It is these first tough years that are the break or make years. You may not make profits during these years and the answer to how long it will take for a business to become profitable isn't always cut and dried. I believe as long as a business is breaking even at least in the first few years then it is growing and it is successful, you just need to keep pushing on.

The secret to a successful business is hard work, integrity, focusing on the opportunity in hand, team work as well as executing your vision. You will not always get it right but you need to learn to push past the feeling of failure. One of the greatest mistakes I made was being unclear about what I stand for and assuming that everyone was automatically going to love my brand. It's great to be passionate about your brand and enthusiastic about the services your brand provides. After all you must first believe in the brand before you sell the concept to others. But always beware of losing perspective. For instance do not go into business assuming that you have no competition and everyone will immediately buy into your great business. That's why you must constantly give your brand visibility by advertising and engaging with clients no matter how many years of success your business has had, as well continue to be innovative in order to remain relevant.

The entrepreneurial journey requires one to be proud of their uniqueness and value and not to try and copy and paste someone else's idea. Be yourself no matter what others think because you are the only one who knows your vision. For your brand to be noticed, remembered and successful it should be unique.

Once a business is successful you need to master the art to handle money and make more. Wealth has to be dealt with care because you can lose it all if not taken care of and if you don't plan it well you will have no growth. Find mentors who can hold your hand as you go along. In addition keep the faith and know that nothing is impossible with God, and that hard work does not kill if you are passionate about what you do. As long as you show up at your business every day and give it your very best, ask God to bless the work of your hands; He is faithful. Know that you need patience too as it takes time for your hard work to pay off but eventually it will.

Timeless Medical Spa staff

Chapter 20

Embrace all your Life's experiences.

I am not what happened to me, I am what I choose to become.
– C.G. Jung

WHEN I RECALL SOME OF my circumstances in life, I know I had every possible reason to fail. Growing up in the village and seeing the face of poverty around you can influence you to think that is all you are destined for in life. There weren't many people you could look up to in the village, if anything ours seemed to be among the affluent ones, according to the standards at the village. But I did not want to limit my dreams to the village. Now, I know for sure that to succeed in life one ought to be open minded and flexible to new experiences and possibilities even when unsure what path to take. You just have to have some faith and trust the process of life. And this is especially important in one's youth, although to be honest it doesn't matter what stage of life you are at. The most important thing is to start now, right where you are with what you have. Do not look at your life and think you have nothing to offer. The story of Moses in the bible is a good example that we all have something within us. Exodus 4:2-5 Then the Lord said to him, "What is that in your hand?" "A rod," he replied. The Lord said, "Throw it on the ground." Moses threw it on the ground and it became a snake, and he ran from it. Then the Lord said to him, "Reach out your hand and take it by the tail." So Moses reached out and took hold of the snake and it turned back into a rod in his hand. What has God put in your hand? This is the very thing that you need to start with, the rest will fall into place as you go on.

I was one of those who did not always know my purpose in life, up until I was 30 years old. And so I tried my knack at many things. I truly did not know where these would lead in life, at least not at the time. But just like I was determined in my teens not to let the life I had lived in the village hinder me from succeeding, I was not going to let my uncertainty regarding my purpose stop me from finding and carving my path in life.

Instead, I used these experiences I had grown up with to push me to dream big. I can confidently say that it was this life of lack; lack of money, lack of clarity that has shaped me into the woman I am today, a testament that one's present circumstances don't determine how far one can go in life. I used my lack as a force to drive myself to succeed in life, there was no other alternative.

I have learnt that despite the challenging situations you may face in life, if you look hard enough, there will be a lesson and an opportunity to transform the challenge into something greater as long as you do not give up.

Life has taught me that you do need to know everything in life for you to succeed. However you need to be a student of life; always curious, always asking questions, more eager to listen than to speak and willing to learn and grow.

And while at it, you need to allow yourself to just experiment even when you are unsure. Either way your experiment can yield two results; success or lessons, and these are both vital in life.

Now older and wiser, I realise that no experience in life is wasted. Yes, even that which you think is the worst you have gone through has made you stronger. So embrace it. You may not like it when you are going through it, it may not even sense at the time, but it will one day. So for now, persevere, stay strong, trudge on. Everything in life always works together to form one beautiful tapestry.

Having a good time at home

About the Author

PERIS MBUTHIA IS A KENYAN entrepreneur who runs a successful medical spa in Nairobi, Kenya. She is married to Martin Mbuthia and together, they have two beautiful daughters, Sandra and Maxine.

Her passion for beauty and health has seen her get involved in the healthcare industry worldwide for over 20 years. She has also been actively involved in the local Kenyan media in promoting and educating people on the importance of skincare.

Peris has lived in the UK, USA and Canada, where she was actively involved in her local church's youth club.

She has put all her gained knowledge and life experience into this book. Her testimony in life is that no dream is too big to be accomplished.

Email: info@perismbuthia.com

Website: www.perismbuthia.com